Spinal cord and Nerves

Injury, Illness and Health

Steve Parker

www.heinemann.co.uk/library
Visit our website to find out more information about **Heinemann Library** books.

To order:
☎ Phone 44 (0) 1865 888066
▤ Send a fax to 44 (0) 1865 314091
▢ Visit the Heinemann Bookshop at www.heinemann.co.uk/library to browse our catalogue and order online.

First published in Great Britain by Heinemann Library, Halley Court, Jordan Hill, Oxford OX2 8EJ, part of Harcourt Education.

Heinemann is a registered trademark of Harcourt Education Ltd.

Editorial: Sarah Eason and Georga Godwin
Design: Jo Hinton-Malivoire and AMR
Illustrations: Art Construction
Picture Research: Rosie Garai and Debra Weatherley
Production: Viv Hichens

Originated by Blenheim Colour Ltd
Printed in China by W K T Co. Ltd

ISBN 0 431 15704 9 (hardback)
07 06 05 04 03
10 9 8 7 6 5 4 3 2 1

ISBN 0 431 15711 1 (paperback)
08 07 06 05 04
10 9 8 7 6 5 4 3 2 1

British Library Cataloguing in Publication Data
Parker, Steve
Spinal cord & nerves. – (Body Focus)
612.8'1
A full catalogue record for this book is available from the British Library.

Acknowledgements
The Publishers would like to thank the following for permission to reproduce photographs:
Actionplus pp. **21**, **37**; AP/Eric Draper p. **33**; Corbis/Bryn Colton/Assignments p. **39**; Getty Images pp. **5**, **13**, **29**; Imaging Body p. **35**; Kit Houghton/Houghton's Horses p. **28**; SPL pp. **31**, **43**; SPL/BSIP, Laurent/Pioffet p. **40**; SPL/David Gifford p. **19**; SPL/Deep Light Productions p. **16**; SPL/Dr John Zajicek p. **38**; SPL/GJP-CNRI p. **15**; SPL/James King-Holmes p. **42**; SPL/John Radcliffe Hospital p. **34**; SPL/Mauro Fermariello p. **30**; SPL/Will & Deni McIntyre p. **25**; Sporting Pictures p. **11**.

The cover coloured three-dimensional computer tomography scan of the front of the lower spine is produced courtesy of Science Photo Library/GJLP.

The Publishers would like to thank David Wright for his assistance with the preparation of this book.

Every effort has been made to contact copyright holders of any material reproduced in this book. Any omissions will be rectified in subsequent printings if notice is given to the Publishers.

Disclaimer
All the internet adresses (URLs) given in the book were valid at the time of going to press. However, due to the dynamic nature of the Internet, some addresses may have changed, or sites may have changed or ceased to exist since publication. While the author and Publishers regret any inconvenience this may cause readers, no responsibility for any such changes can be accepted by either the author or the Publishers.

CONTENTS

Words appearing in the text in bold, **like this**, are explained in the Glossary.

THE NERVOUS SYSTEM

The human body contains hundreds of different parts, such as the stomach, intestines, liver, kidneys, brain, bones, muscles and heart. Each has its own tasks to do. However, all parts must work together, in a controlled and coordinated way, so that the body can function as a whole and stay healthy.

Controlling the body

Two systems in the body control all of its parts, ensuring that they work together. They are the nervous system and the hormonal system. The nervous system has three main parts – the brain, the spinal cord and the nerves. This book focuses on the 'non-brain' parts of the nervous system – the spinal cord and the nerves.

brain

autonomic
nerves

spinal
cord

peripheral
nerves

Two similar systems

In some ways, the body's nervous system is similar to the telephone system that we use daily to make calls, send e-mails and surf the Internet. Both the nervous system and the telephone system are designed in the form of a network, with millions of senders, receivers and connections. Both are designed to send information or messages from one place to another. In both systems, the messages travel in the form of tiny electrical signals or pulses, along bundles of long, wire-like structures. In both systems, there are parts called relay stations, which pass information on to its destination.

The nervous system has three main parts: the brain in the head, the spinal cord extending down the back and the peripheral nerves throughout the body.

The entire nervous system is really made up of three systems that work together as a whole, as described below.

Central nervous system

The central nervous system (CNS) consists of the brain and spinal cord. The brain is the most important part, because it is the site of our thoughts, feelings, emotions, desires, ideas and memories. The spinal cord links the brain to many parts of the body.

Peripheral nervous system

The **peripheral** nervous system (PNS) is the network of nerves that branch from the brain and spinal cord to every body part. They carry messages around the body, to and from the brain and spinal cord. Some of these messages are about sensations, such as what the eyes see or what the skin touches. Other messages are about body movements that are **voluntary** – those we make at will, and that we can control by our thoughts.

The third part of the nervous system is the **autonomic** nervous system (ANS). This deals with autonomic, or 'automatic', body processes. These are **involuntary** – that is, they happen on their own, without our awareness or need to think about them. They include heartbeat, digestion and removal of wastes.

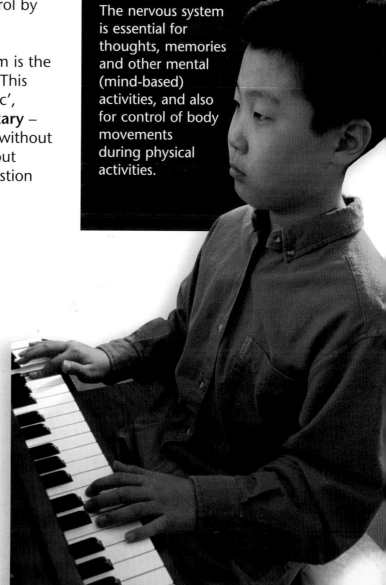

The nervous system is essential for thoughts, memories and other mental (mind-based) activities, and also for control of body movements during physical activities.

Neurology

The medical study of the brain, spinal cord and nerves, how they work and the disorders that affect them is known as neurology. A neurologist is a doctor who specializes in problems of the nervous system. A neurosurgeon carries out operations on these parts.

NERVE CELLS

The nervous system is made up of more than 100 billion nerve **cells**, called neurons. Most are in the brain and spinal cord. Compared to other types of cells, they live for a very long time. Skin cells, for example, live only for about one month and blood cells live for three months. However, nerve cells last for many years.

Features of a nerve cell

A typical nerve cell has three main parts – **cell body**, **dendrites** and **axon** (fibre).

The cell body is much the same as other cells. It has a control centre, or **nucleus**, and other normal cell parts. In most nerve cells, the cell body is about 20–30 micrometres (1/50th to 1/30th of a millimetre) across.

Dendrites

Dendrites are long, thin branches that grow from the cell body. They extend outwards like a spider's web, branching and becoming thinner. They are so long that their ends almost touch other nerve cells. The main task of the dendrites is to receive nerve messages from other nerve cells, and to carry them towards the cell body.

Axons (fibres)

The nerve fibre is a long, thick, wire-like branch of the cell body. It may have its own finger-like branches at its end, the fibre terminal. The main task of the fibre is to carry nerve messages away from the cell body, and to pass them to other nerve cells.

A nerve cell (neuron) has a cell body similar to other cells, but also long extensions called dendrites and an even longer axon or nerve fibre.

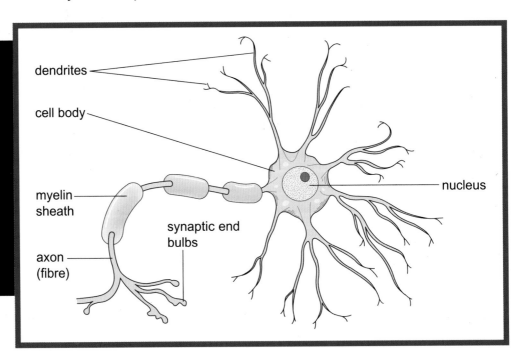

dendrites

cell body

myelin sheath

synaptic end bulbs

axon (fibre)

nucleus

Nerve cells have many designs. Some have very short fibres, or several fibres. Some have just a few dendrites, while others have thousands. Some have a cell body that is found halfway along the fibre, rather than near one end.

Types of nerve fibres

There are two main kinds of nerve fibres: myelinated and un-myelinated.

A myelinated fibre has a covering, or sheath, wrapped around it. This sheath is made of a special kind of cell, called the Schwann cell (neurolemmocyte). As the Schwann cell grows, it wraps itself around the fibre several times, like rolling a sheet of plastic around a long pole. The outer layer, or **membrane**, of the Schwann cell makes a fatty substance, called **myelin**.

The myelin sheath works like the plastic coating on an electric wire. It stops a nerve signal from leaking away or becoming weaker as it passes along the fibre. It also helps the nerve signal to travel faster along the fibre – 100 metres per second or even more.

One myelin sheath does not usually stretch the whole length of the fibre. There are several sheaths, one after another, separated by tiny gaps, called nodes. A nerve signal travels fastest between these nodes, 'jumping' from one to the next.

An un-myelinated fibre has no covering of myelin. It carries nerve messages more slowly, usually at about 1 to 2 metres per second.

Most nerve fibres in the spinal cord and **peripheral** nerves are myelinated. In the brain, many fibres are un-myelinated.

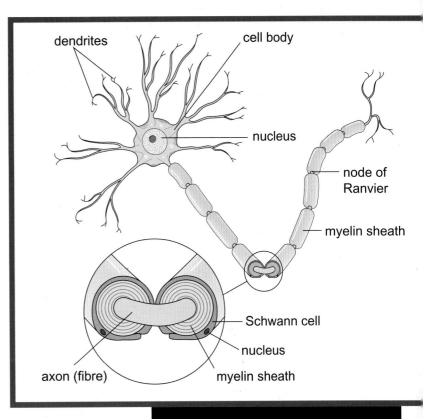

dendrites
cell body
nucleus
node of Ranvier
myelin sheath
Schwann cell
nucleus
axon (fibre)
myelin sheath

A myelinated nerve fibre has a series of coverings called myelin sheaths around its axon (fibre). Each myelin sheath is a single cell, called a Schwann cell. It grows in a spiral fashion around the fibre, and contains the fatty substance called myelin. The dendrites do not have coverings.

The longest cells

Some nerve cell fibres, in the nerves of the arms and legs, are more than 60 centimetres in length. These nerve cells are by far the longest cells in the body. Despite their length, each single fibre is far too thin to see with the unaided eye.

INSIDE A NERVE

A typical nerve looks pale grey or whitish in colour, and is smooth and shiny. The thickest **peripheral** nerve is the sciatic nerve, which is found in the hip and upper leg. It is nearly as wide as a thumb. The thinnest peripheral nerves are as narrow as hairs. Thick or thin, most nerves have the same basic structure.

Outer covering

A nerve has a tough, **fibrous** outer covering, or sheath. This protects it from being twisted, kinked or squashed. Inside the nerve are long **axons** (fibres), each from a single nerve **cell**. A thick main nerve has hundreds of thousands of fibres. Very small and thin nerves, such as those that control the small muscles that move the eyeball, have just a few dozen fibres.

Bundles of fibres

The fibres are grouped into bundles (fascicles). Usually, the fibres in one bundle are all **sensory** or all **motor**. Some nerves contain only bundles of motor fibres, and are called motor nerves. Others contain only sensory fibres, and are known as sensory nerves. However, many nerves are mixed, with some bundles of sensory fibres and some bundles of motor fibres.

In addition to nerve fibres, most nerves also contain tiny **blood vessels** that supply nourishment and take away wastes. They also have a fatty substance that provides 'padding', like cushioning, between and around the bundles.

Ganglia

Along many nerves are lump-like bulges, known as **ganglia**. These are collections of nerve cell bodies, whose fibres pass along the main length of the nerve. The nerve cell bodies are surrounded by 'satellite' cells, which pass nourishment to them and take away their wastes. Ganglia also contain supporting fibres and tiny blood vessels.

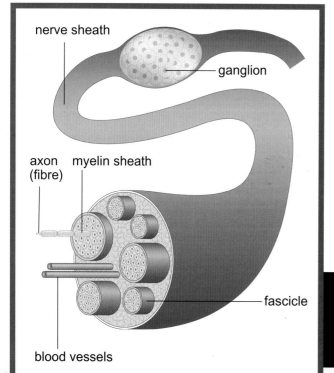

nerve sheath

ganglion

axon (fibre)

myelin sheath

fascicle

blood vessels

A typical nerve contains several bundles of long nerve axons (fibres), wrapped in tough coverings known as fascicles.

'Gone to sleep'

Sometimes, we sit or lie in an awkward position, with one part of the body pressing on another, or with a joint bent in an unusual way. This can squash a nerve or its blood supply, which stops the nerve from working normally. Numbness or loss of feeling, and perhaps aching, warn of the problem. The part may not be able to move. When this occurs, we say the body part has 'gone to sleep'.

'Pins and needles'

After a body part has 'gone to sleep', we stretch or move it to relieve the problem. The nerve and its blood supply begin to work again, giving a tingling, or 'pins and needles', sensation as the nerve signals start to pass along it. Rubbing the part and flexing its joints also help to speed up recovery.

Naming nerves

Individual nerves are usually named after the part of the body they pass through, or from the name of a nearby muscle or bone. For example, the ulnar nerve runs down the inner side of the arm. It is named after the ulna, the bone in the lower arm along which it lies.

Each branch of each main nerve also has its own name. As a result, there are hundreds of medical names, one for each of the body's peripheral nerves.

In most human bodies, the main nerves follow a similar branching pattern into the major body parts and organs. However, there is variation among individual people in the length and branching of the smaller nerves.

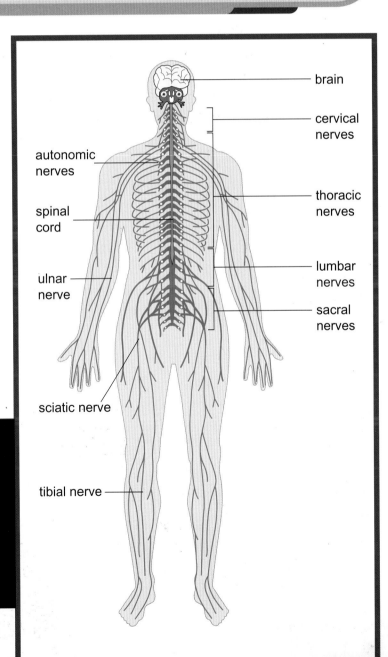

- brain
- cervical nerves
- autonomic nerves
- thoracic nerves
- spinal cord
- ulnar nerve
- lumbar nerves
- sacral nerves
- sciatic nerve
- tibial nerve

HOW NERVE SIGNALS WORK

Every second, millions of nerve signals pass through the body's nervous system – especially up and down the spinal cord, and around the brain. A single nerve signal is a tiny, brief pulse of electricity. It has the strength of about 0.1 volts (a standard torch battery is 1.5 volts). It lasts only about 1 millisecond – that is, one-thousandth of a second.

At the membrane

A nerve signal does not pass along the inside of a nerve **cell**. It passes along its outer layer, or cell **membrane**. The signal is made by the movement of substances called **ions**. These are natural body chemicals, dissolved and floating in the watery liquid on both sides of the cell membrane. Because these substances are dissolved, they have charges – they are either positive or negative. The main ones are sodium and potassium, which both have positive charges.

The nerve cell's membrane has tiny structures in it, called ion pumps. These pass, or 'push', certain ions through the membrane, which normally acts as a barrier. The movements of the charged ions across the cell membrane make a nerve signal, as shown on the diagram here.

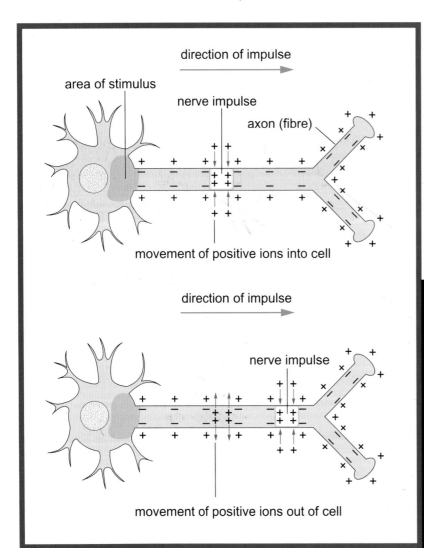

direction of impulse

area of stimulus

nerve impulse

axon (fibre)

movement of positive ions into cell

direction of impulse

nerve impulse

movement of positive ions out of cell

A nerve signal, or impulse, is a tiny burst of electricity formed by the movements of dissolved substances called ions. These pass into and out of the nerve cell, across its outer covering or membrane. The main ions are sodium and potassium, which are positive. This process is chemical rather than physical, but it still uses energy.

The nerve pulse

When there is no nerve signal, there are more sodium ions outside the cell membrane, in the fluid around the nerve cell. There are also more potassium ions on the other side, which is the fluid inside the nerve cell.

As a nerve signal arrives at a region of cell membrane, sodium pumps push sodium ions from outside the nerve cell to inside the cell. Then, potassium pumps push potassium ions from inside the cell to outside. These rapid movements of positive ions cause a 'spike' of electricity, known as the action potential, which is the nerve signal.

The next region of membrane does the same, and the next, and so on. This makes the message travel along the nerve cell's membrane as a 'wave' of moving ions, which create a flowing electrical pulse.

As people stand and lift arms, then sit, a 'Mexican wave' passes along. In a similar way, ions move in and out of a nerve cell to form the 'moving wave' of a nerve signal.

A moving wave

The movement of sodium ions across the membrane of the nerve cell is called depolarization. The travelling nerve signal is called a wave of depolarization. After it passes, the ions move more slowly, back to their normal positions. During this time, called the refractory period, no signal can pass through the cell.

Most nerve cells carry a few nerve signals each second, even when they have no information to send. As they send more information, they carry more signals closer together – up to 300 per second.

The size of a nerve cell

The **dendrites** and fibres of a nerve cell can be very long indeed. If a nerve cell body was enlarged to the size of a football, then the branching 'web' of dendrites could be big enough to fill a house. The fibre might be much longer – more than one kilometre in length.

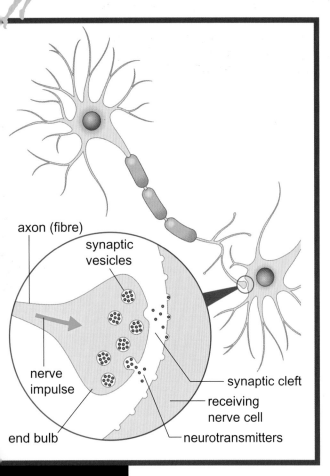

axon (fibre)

synaptic vesicles

nerve impulse

end bulb

synaptic cleft

receiving nerve cell

neurotransmitters

The circle in this diagram shows an enlarged view of the synapse between two nerve cells. A tiny gap, the synaptic cleft, separates the cells.

Nerve **cells** carry nerve messages as tiny electrical signals, and pass them to other nerve cells. However, nerve cells do not actually touch each other. They are separated by tiny gaps, called **synapses**. Nerve messages pass, or 'jump', across the gaps not as waves of electricity, but as body chemicals.

A gap in the way

At the nerve junction, or synapse, the cell **membranes** of two nerve cells are separated by a tiny gap, about one-hundredth of the width of a human hair. It is wide enough to prevent the passage of the 'wave' of electricity of a nerve message.

When the electrical pulse reaches the synapse, it causes the release of chemicals known as **neurotransmitters**. These flow across the gap from the sending nerve cell, and touch the membrane of the receiving nerve cell. The chemicals slot into special 'landing sites', called **receptors**. This alters the receiving membrane in such a way that the original wave of electricity begins again. The whole process is very quick; it only takes about one-thousandth of a second.

Go and stop

Sometimes a receiving nerve cell 'fires' its own nerve signal after it receives just one pulse from a sending nerve cell. In other cases, it only fires its own signal after receiving several nerve pulses in quick succession, either from one sending nerve cell or from several. This effect is called summation.

Instead of telling the receiving nerve cell to fire, some nerve signals actually prevent it from firing. These are known as inhibitory signals, rather than excitatory signals.

In addition, a nerve cell does not simply pass on its messages to one other nerve cell. Most nerve cells have hundreds, even thousands, of synapses, with hundreds or thousands of other nerve cells. So the possible pathways for nerve messages between nerve cells are almost endless.

In a relay race, the baton is passed from one runner to the next. Nerve cells also pass on, or relay, their messages from one to another.

Types of neurotransmitters

So far, medical scientists have discovered more than 50 body chemicals that work as neurotransmitters. The real number could be far higher. Several neurotransmitters in the spinal cord and **peripheral** nerve types are shown in the chart below. They are important because some medical drugs copy or block their effects, and so help to treat problems with the nervous system.

Acetylcholine:
- main neurotransmitter for the peripheral nervous system
- present where a nerve joins to a muscle, at the neuromuscular junction (**motor** end plate)
- drugs that block acetylcholine are used to damp down unwanted muscle action, and to widen the pupils during eye examination.

Glycine:
- has mainly an inhibitory effect, damping down nerve signals that are less important in the spinal cord
- allows important nerve signals to be sent to and from the brain.

Noradrenaline (norepinephrine):
- occurs both in the nervous system, including control of internal processes, such as production of body heat, and also acts as a hormone
- involved in the body's general level of arousal or awareness
- also involved in the nerves of the **autonomic**, or 'automatic', nervous system.

Endorphins:
- occur especially in the spinal cord
- damp down, or inhibit, nerve cells that carry nerve signals for pain
- some painkilling medical drugs are based on endorphins, blocking pain signals passing up the spinal cord.

SPINAL CORD AND SPINAL COLUMN

The spinal cord is the main link between the brain and the body. It is almost a long, thin extension of the brain itself, and is the largest single nerve in the body. The cord is inside a tunnel, called the vertebral tunnel, within the backbone, or spinal column. This tunnel is made of a row of holes; each hole goes through one of the vertebral bones (backbones) of the spinal column.

In an average-sized adult, the spinal cord is about 45 centimetres long and about one centimetre in diameter – similar to the width of a little finger.

The body's main nerve

Along its length, the spinal cord joins with 31 pairs of spinal nerves (see page 22). These branch outwards from the spinal cord into the body, carrying nerve messages to and fro between the spinal cord and hundreds of body parts.

At its upper end, the spinal cord merges with the base of the brain. At its lower end, the spinal cord does not run down to the base of the spinal column. It tapers to a pointed end higher up, at about the level of the navel. Spinal nerves from the lower portion of the cord then run down through the rest of the vertebral tunnel to the base of the spinal column. They branch outwards to the lower body, hips and legs.

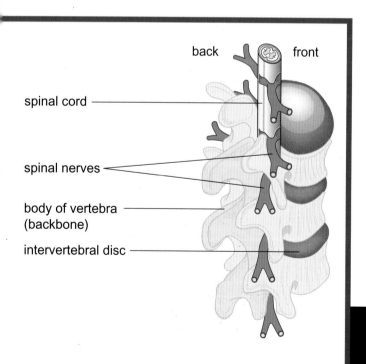

back | front

spinal cord

spinal nerves

body of vertebra
(backbone)

intervertebral disc

Joints in the backbone

Each pair of spinal nerves joins the spinal cord at a small gap between two of the vertebral bones that make up the backbone. The gap is formed where the bones are linked at a joint. Between the two bones, there is a cushion-like pad of tough, but slightly flexible, **cartilage** (gristle). This is known as an intervertebral disc. It holds the two vertebral bones slightly apart, creating the gap for spinal nerves to join the spinal cord.

The spinal cord is inside the spinal column, in a row of holes through the backbones.

In this side view of the backbone, a disc between the vertebrae (individual spine bones) has become misshapen and presses on the spinal cord, causing much pain and partial paralysis.

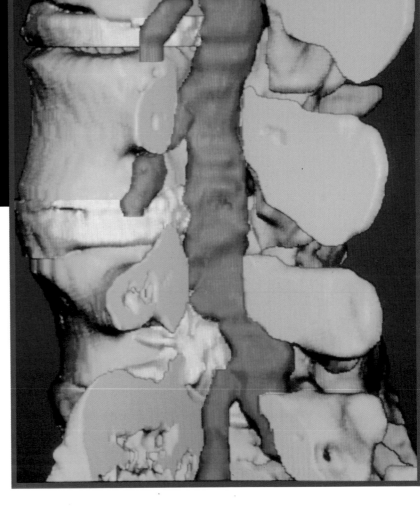

Discs in the backbone

The intervertebral disc allows the two vertebral bones to tilt, or twist, slightly. Over the whole length of the backbone, the small movements at each of these joints work together, so that the neck and back can twist and bend.

The spinal cord is well protected within the spinal column, safe from knocks, twists, kinks and pressure. However, sometimes a disc can press on a spinal nerve and cause problems.

Prolapsed, or 'slipped', disc

The intervertebral disc between two vertebral bones may be weak for some reason, such as a back injury. Or it can become excessively squeezed, for example, when a person suddenly carries very heavy weights. The disc may bulge, or prolapse, at a weak point. The bulge may press on a spinal nerve, or on the spinal cord itself. This can cause pain, and perhaps numbness or weakness of the parts supplied by that nerve. The problem is sometimes called 'slipped disc', but this name is misleading. It is very rare for the whole disc to slip out of position. Usually, the problem is due to the bulge or prolapse.

PROTECTING THE SPINAL CORD AND NERVES

When some parts of the body are injured or diseased, they can repair themselves. For example, a scrape on the skin soon heals as new skin forms. Nerve **cells**, however, have very complicated shapes and millions of delicate connections. They are so specialized that they cannot normally multiply, to replace themselves, as part of everyday body maintenance. As a result, the natural process of repair to the nervous system is very slow and, in some cases, it may not be possible at all.

Long-term outlook

The long-term nature of nerve damage means that it is vitally important to avoid injury or harm, especially to the brain, spinal cord and nerves. Injury can happen just as easily on a short car journey as in extreme sports such as snowboarding and skydiving. The alternative to taking care may be a broken neck or back, with far-reaching effects on daily life.

Care and precautions

One of the main precautions is to make full use of protective clothing and equipment. This includes helmets, visors and head guards, neck and back braces, shoulder and hip pads, elbow and knee guards, wrist strengtheners, gloves, shin guards (as in soccer) and ankle and foot protectors.

This equipment is designed to prevent all kinds of injury, from wounds, sprained joints and broken bones to trapped or crushed nerves, and a broken neck or back. Some cases of nerve damage happen when a body part is pulled or wrenched violently, and a bone or joint crushes a nearby nerve.

Serious back injury can be caused by a fall from a cliff face – or even off a chair.

Carpal tunnel syndrome

Carpal tunnel syndrome affects a nerve in the wrist called the median nerve. This nerve runs through a 'tunnel', formed by the bones of the wrist and a strong band, the carpal ligament, which wraps around the inside of the wrist like a watch strap.

The median nerve may be squeezed, or compressed, due to a wrist injury, or to a disorder that affects the joint, such as arthritis. Another cause is tendinitis. The long tendons of the forearm muscles pass through the wrist to move the fingers. These tendons may become sore, swollen and painful in people who use their fingers every day in repeated actions, such as typing at a computer keyboard.

Compression of the median nerve produces tingling and numbness in parts of the hand. It may cause pain that becomes worse at night. It can also make delicate finger movements difficult. Treatment varies from rest or **anti-inflammatory** injections to loosening the carpal ligament by an operation.

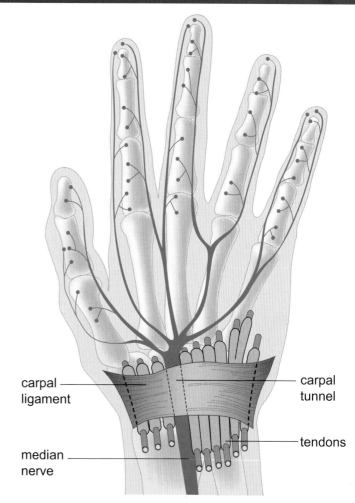

carpal ligament

carpal tunnel

tendons

median nerve

The main nerve in the wrist passes through a gap or 'tunnel', under the strap-like carpal ligament and between muscle tendons to the hand. In carpal tunnel syndrome, the nerve is put under pressure and becomes inflamed.

Training and coaching

For almost any sort of activity, the right kind of training routine can help to prevent injury. Training strengthens muscles and joints, and it teaches movement control. This makes accidents, sprains, strains and nerve damage less likely. A coach or supervisor can also explain the dangers and hazards of an activity. He or she can advise on how to get out of a dangerous situation with the least harm – for example, how to fall properly and avoid an injury.

The spinal cord is narrower than its tunnel-like hole within the bones of the spinal column. Filling the space between the outside of the cord and the inside of the bony tunnel are three sheet-like layers, called **meninges**. They wrap around the spinal cord like three long bags, one inside the other. At the upper end of the spinal cord, where it merges with the brain, the meninges continue and wrap around the brain itself.

The three layers of the meninges form a 'cushion' around the spinal cord – almost like wrapping a valuable item in foamed-rubber or spongy plastic. The meninges protect the cord from sudden knocks, kinks, twists and jars, inside its tunnel within the backbone.

The meninges wrap around the spinal cord along its length. The outer one nearest the backbone is the dura mater. The middle one, with extensive blood vessels, is the arachnoid. There is a fluid-filled gap between it and the inner one, covering the cord itself, the pia mater.

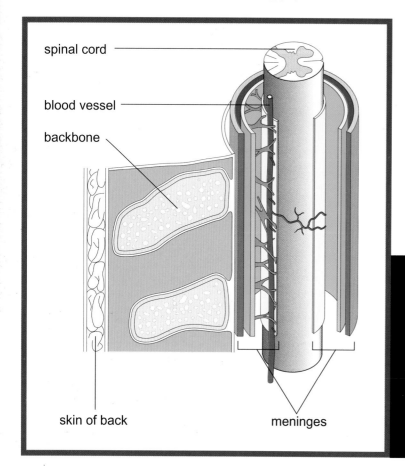

spinal cord

blood vessel

backbone

skin of back

meninges

Fluid around the cord

There is a slight gap between the middle and the innermost of the three meninges. This is not an empty space, however. It contains a special liquid, known as cerebrospinal fluid, or CSF. This fluid also fills the central canal, which is the tiny hole along the middle of the spinal cord.

The meninges extend above the spinal cord and around the brain. The CSF also extends around the brain. In fact, it is made inside the brain, at the rate of a few teaspoonfuls each day. The fluid oozes in a slow, one-way flow, around the brain and down around the spinal cord. It seeps slowly out through the meninges, at the same rate it is made, and into the general **blood vessels** nearby.

What does cerebrospinal fluid do?

CSF contains substances that nourish the spinal cord, including oxygen and various **minerals**. It also contains germ-fighting white blood cells, and it collects waste substances from around the spinal cord, which it carries away into the blood.

In addition, the CSF helps the meninges to protect the spinal cord. It forms a 'water-cushion' around the spinal cord to protect it from sudden knocks and jarring.

Importance of CSF

Unusual substances in CSF can suggest certain health problems:

- increased **gamma globulin** (a type of body protein) in CSF may indicate multiple sclerosis
- the presence of blood in CSF may indicate a bleed, or **haemorrhage**, around the brain or spinal cord
- certain germs in CSF can confirm an infection, such as meningitis.

A small sample of cerebrospinal fluid may be taken for tests, by the procedure called lumbar puncture (see panel).

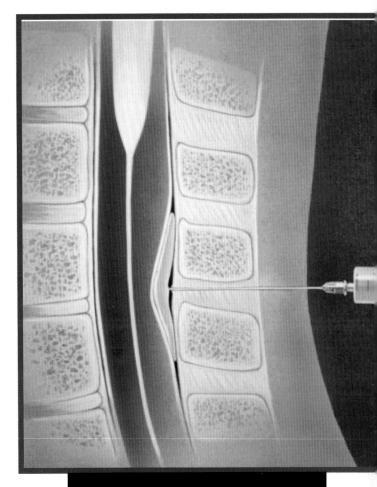

This illustration shows an epidural taking place. A needle is inserted between two vertebrae to inject an anaesthetic.

Lumbar puncture

A small sample of cerebrospinal fluid is usually taken by lumbar puncture, or 'spinal tap'. A hollow needle is inserted, with great care, through the skin and muscles of the lower back (the lumbar spine), and between two vertebral bones, into the meninges. A sample of CSF is withdrawn into a syringe for tests. A similar procedure, known as epidural anaesthetic, is used to inject drugs that relieve pain during childbirth, or during an operation on the lower body.

From the outside, the spinal cord looks pale grey in colour, with pairs of similar-coloured nerves branching from it. Inside the spinal cord, there is an H-shaped darker area in the centre, surrounded by a much paler area. These two areas are known as grey and white matter and, under the microscope, they look very different.

Grey and white matter

The H-shaped area of grey matter is actually pinkish-grey in colour. It contains the main parts, or **cell bodies**, of nerve **cells**, along with their short, spider-like connections, known as **dendrites**. There are very few nerve fibres (**axons**).

In the grey matter, nerve messages are passed between nerve cells. They are routed to and fro, as they arrive from the brain above and then go out to body parts along the spinal nerves, or as they come in from body parts to be sent up to the brain.

White matter contains mainly long, wire-like fibres. These are nerve 'highways', which carry the tiny electrical pulses that make up nerve messages.

Compared to a telephone system, the white matter is like the bundles of electric cables or optical fibres, which carry messages at high speed over long distances. The grey matter is like a mixture of telephones, computers and exchanges, where the messages are sent and received, sorted out and processed.

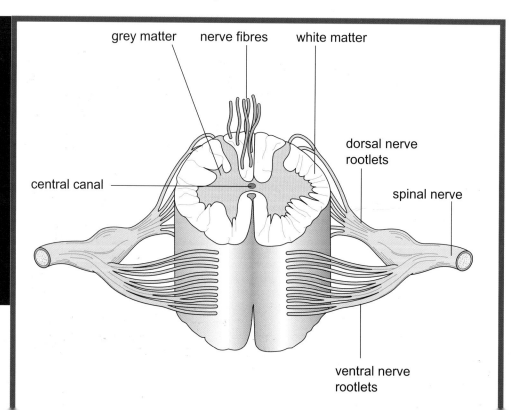

This cut-through view of the spinal cord shows a central area of grey matter, surrounded by white matter of nerve fibres.

grey matter   nerve fibres   white matter

dorsal nerve rootlets

central canal

spinal nerve

ventral nerve rootlets

Sensory signals

All nerve messages are made up of tiny electrical signals. There are two kinds of nerve messages, depending on where they are going.

Sensory messages come from the body's sense organs and parts, and go to the brain. The sensory parts include the eyes, ears, nose, tongue and skin. There are also sensors inside the body, which detect temperature, blood pressure and other conditions.

Motor signals

Motor messages travel in the opposite way – from the brain, out into the body. Most are sent to muscles, telling them when to pull and by how much, so that the body can move. Other motor messages control the heart, intestines and other internal parts. Also, some motor messages travel to body parts called **glands**. They control the release of contents from the gland, such as saliva (spit) from the salivary glands in the face.

White matter and nerve tracts

In the spinal cord's white matter, the nerve fibres are found in bundles, or groups, called tracts:

- ascending tracts carry sensory messages that come from spinal nerves, up the spinal cord to the brain
- descending tracts convey motor messages from the brain, down the spinal cord and then out along spinal nerves to muscles and glands.

In fast sports, such as table tennis, nerve signals flash up and down the spinal cord, between the brain and the body, at the rate of millions every second.

PERIPHERAL NERVES

There are 31 pairs of spinal nerves that branch from each side of the spinal cord. These nerves snake out through the body, dividing into smaller and smaller branches, which reach into every part of the body – from the top of the head to the tips of the fingers and toes.

This huge and complicated network of nerves is called the **peripheral** nervous system. It is estimated that if all the peripheral nerves from one body were joined end to end, they would circle the Earth three times!

Where the nerves go

There are five main groups of spinal nerve pairs. The eight pairs of cervical spinal nerves lead out from the upper part of the spinal cord. They go to the neck, shoulder and outside part of the arm. Twelve pairs of thoracic spinal nerves curve around the front and back of the chest, between the ribs and along the inside part of the arm. Five pairs of lumbar spinal nerves branch out into the small of the back, the hips and the front and side of each leg. Five pairs of sacral spinal nerves lead to the groin, buttocks and the back of each leg and ankle. The single pair of coccygeal spinal nerves, at the base of the spinal cord, go to a small part of the groin and buttock area.

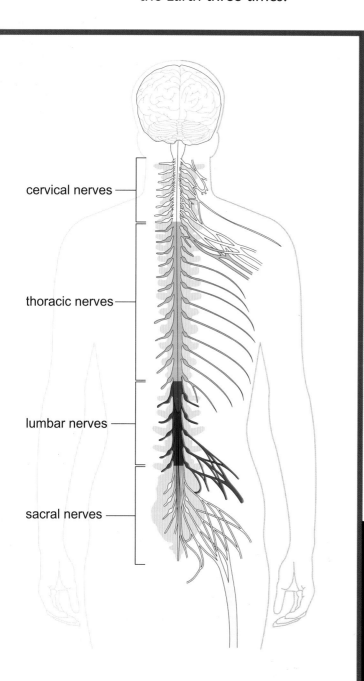

cervical nerves

thoracic nerves

lumbar nerves

sacral nerves

The main groups of spinal nerves are named after the body parts they branch into, such as the thoracic nerves, which spread into the thorax or chest. The sacral nerves branch out from the sacrum, which is the rear part of the hip bone or pelvis.

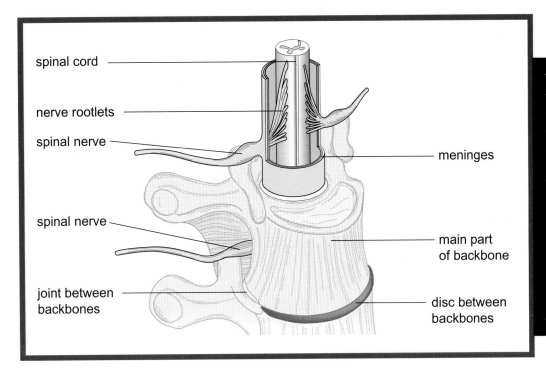

spinal cord

nerve rootlets

spinal nerve

meninges

spinal nerve

main part
of backbone

joint between
backbones

disc between
backbones

Nerve roots

Near the spinal cord, each spinal nerve divides into two main parts, called nerve roots. The dorsal nerve root arches round to the rear of the spinal cord, while the ventral nerve root curves round to the front.

Within about one centimetre of the spinal cord, each spinal nerve root divides into many smaller rootlets, like the fingers of a tiny hand. It is these rootlets that merge into the spinal cord.

The two roots of each spinal nerve carry different messages. The dorsal (back) nerve root conveys **sensory** nerve signals into the spinal cord, mainly from the skin. The ventral (front) nerve root carries **motor** nerve signals out from the spinal cord to the muscles and **glands**.

Cranial nerves

The peripheral nervous system also includes twelve pairs of cranial nerves. These branch out from the brain itself, rather than from the spinal cord. They connect the brain directly to the main sense organs in the head – the eyes, ears, nose, mouth and skin. They also link the brain directly to muscles in the face, head and neck, including the muscles for speaking and swallowing. One cranial nerve, called the vagus, has branches that pass down through the neck to parts in the main body, such as the heart and stomach.

The brain does not control every movement that the body makes. The spinal cord and **peripheral** nerves can work on their own, to receive nerve signals from **sensory** parts, and then send out signals to muscles to tell them to carry out a movement. These actions usually take place automatically, without the involvement of the brain, although the brain may become aware of them a second or two later. Such rapid, automatic reactions are called **reflexes**.

Withdrawal reflex

There are more than twenty common examples of reflex actions. In the withdrawal reflex, pain or an unusual sensation in the fingers or hand causes the arm to suddenly pull away. For example, if the fingers touch something hot, the hand is quickly jerked away. The same happens in the leg, if the toes or foot sense pain.

These reflex reactions help to protect the body from harm or injury. Even if the brain is busy thinking about something else, such as what the eyes see, the body still reacts in a split second, and the reflex reduces damage.

Stretch reflexes

Several reflexes help us to stand and walk, almost without thinking. Usually, we are not aware of these reflexes unless one is tested on its own. An example is the knee-jerk (patellar) reflex. To test this reflex, a person sits up, with one knee crossed over the other, and the upper knee is tapped just below the kneecap. This stretches the tendon under the skin. The reflex response is for the thigh muscles to straighten the knee, making the foot 'kick out'. This reflex occurs naturally if the knee suddenly bends or sags when the body is supposed to be standing upright. The reflex response straightens the knee to support the body firmly again.

In the patellar, or knee-jerk, reflex a sensory nerve cell sends messages direct to a motor nerve cell.

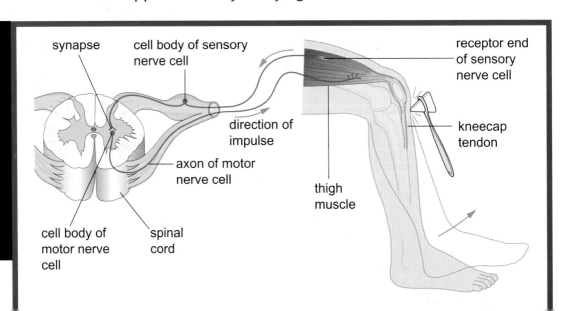

synapse

cell body of sensory nerve cell

receptor end of sensory nerve cell

direction of impulse

kneecap tendon

axon of motor nerve cell

thigh muscle

cell body of motor nerve cell

spinal cord

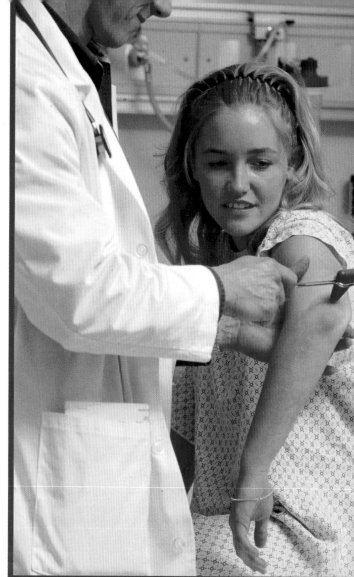

Testing reflexes

Testing reflexes can provide a doctor with valuable information about nerve system damage or other problems. For example, if the knee-jerk reflex does not work properly, this may suggest damage to the spinal cord in the lower back. A similar reflex occurs at the elbow when this is tapped. If this reflex does not work properly, there may be spinal cord or nerve damage in the neck area.

Reflex pathways

A typical reflex involves two or three sets of nerve cells. The first set is sensory nerve cells. They detect a change, for example, a painful sensation in the skin, and send signals along their peripheral nerve, into the spinal cord.

The elbow-jerk reflex is one that can be easily tested. The body has many other reflexes, too – in the hands and feet, limbs and back, and even in the eyes.

Inside the spinal cord, there may be a second set of nerve cells, called interneurons. These receive the incoming sensory messages and relay or pass them onwards to **motor** nerve cells. In most cases, interneurons also send messages up the spinal cord to the brain. This makes us aware that the reflex is happening, although we cannot stop or control it.

The third set is motor nerve cells. They convey nerve signals from the spinal cord, out to the muscles that carry out the movement. If there are no interneurons, signals pass straight from the sensory nerve cells to the motor nerve cells, inside the spinal cord.

AUTONOMIC NERVOUS SYSTEM

If we had to remember to make our heart beat, our lungs breathe and our stomach churn every second of every day, we would have no time for other thoughts. The brain would be 'overloaded' with the basic processes of staying alive.

The **autonomic** nervous system (ANS) could be called the 'automatic' nervous system. It takes care of basic activities inside the body, which keep us alive. This leaves our minds free for more interesting thoughts.

What the system does

The autonomic nervous system includes parts of the **peripheral** nervous system, and uses many of the same nerves. It is basically a **motor** system. It carries messages from the brain to all body parts. The body processes it controls are **involuntary** – that is, we do not have to think about controlling them. They happen without our conscious awareness.

The autonomic nervous system keeps processes inside the body running smoothly, and body conditions constant. This is known as **homeostasis**. In these tasks, the autonomic nervous system is helped by the hormonal system (see panel on page 27). The processes it controls include:

- heartbeat, especially rate and volume of blood
- flow of blood around the body in the **blood vessels**
- muscular motions of the stomach and intestines during digestion
- breathing, especially the width of the main airways in the lungs
- removal of wastes from the blood by the kidneys and bladder
- release from various **glands** of their products, such as saliva (spit), tear fluid for the eyes, sweat on the skin and digestive juices in the intestines
- the size of the pupil, the round opening at the front of each eye, which lets light into the eye.

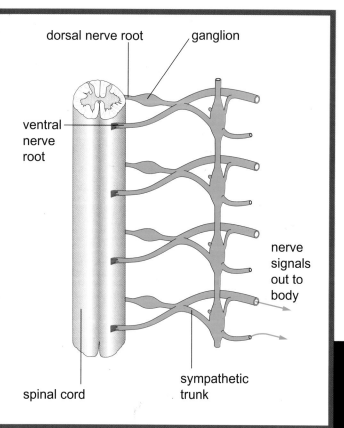

dorsal nerve root   ganglion

ventral nerve root

nerve signals out to body

spinal cord

sympathetic trunk

The autonomic nervous system includes long nerve-like parts called sympathetic trunks, which have lumps known as ganglia along them.

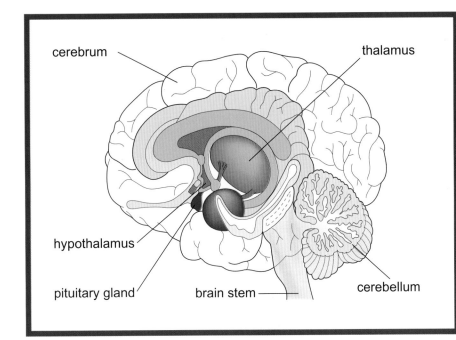

cerebrum

thalamus

hypothalamus

pituitary gland

brain stem

cerebellum

Control of the autonomic nervous system

The part of the brain called the **hypothalamus** is the body's 'automatic pilot'. It has overall control of the autonomic nervous system. The system itself consists of two sets of nerve pathways, known as the sympathetic and parasympathetic divisions. In many cases, these control the same body parts, but they act in opposite, or 'push-pull', ways.

Pushing and pulling

The sympathetic division is 'push', or stimulatory. It makes body parts more active during times of **stress** and action, when rapid response and urgent reactions may be needed. For example, it speeds up heartbeat, widens the eye's pupils and works with **hormones** to provide extra high-energy glucose sugar in the blood flowing to muscles.

The parasympathetic division is 'pull', or inhibitory. It acts against the sympathetic division to damp down body parts and processes, and to restore a slower, calm, resting state.

Between them, the two divisions of the autonomic nervous system fine-tune the body inside to suit conditions outside.

The hormonal system

The hormonal, or endocrine, system is the body's second control and coordination system. It works closely with the nervous system. In general, the nervous system works over short time scales for movements – split seconds, seconds and minutes. The hormonal system works on a longer time scale, for processes that take hours, days and even years, such as growth and sexual development.

The spinal cord is one of the best-protected parts of the body. It is inside a tunnel within the backbone. In turn, the backbone is surrounded by muscles, tendons and other parts, giving strength and stability. Despite these layers of protection, in rare cases, the spinal cord can be injured. In the UK, spinal cord injury accounts for about one emergency hospital visit in 5,000. In the USA, there are about 10,000 such cases each year.

Main causes

Road traffic accidents are the most common cause of spinal injury. Falls are the second. Sometimes, the forces involved in these events are too strong for the backbone, muscles and other protection to withstand. The spinal cord can be severely bent, kinked, torn or even broken if two of the bones in the neck or back slip, one across the other. The parts of the body affected depend on the site or level of the injury (see page 32).

Falls and collisions

In a fall from a height, the body's own weight can severely bend or crack the backbone. This may occur at one of the joints, where the vertebral bones, or the discs between them, cannot cope with the stress involved. They shatter, and the pieces press on, or into, the spinal cord and its nerve roots.

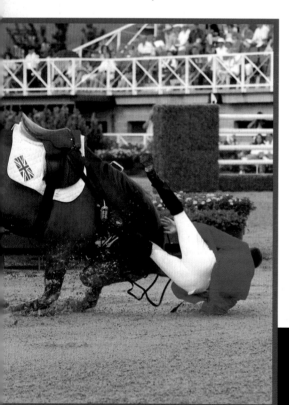

Other causes of spinal cord damage include sports injuries, stab wounds, gunshot wounds and a very weak backbone, due to diseases such as bone cancer.

Rarely, players collide during sport and cause a spinal cord injury. This tends to happen when one player is moving fast and suddenly crashes into another player, or players. This is especially common when the head takes the force of the crash, or when one player's neck or back becomes twisted by the weight and actions of another player. This is why suitable clothing, and head and body protection are so important.

This showjumper has fallen off his horse. However, no injuries occured because he had been taught how to fall safely.

Whiplash

One of the most common spinal cord injuries is 'whiplash', caused during a traffic accident. The person's body, held by a seat belt, comes to a sudden halt with the vehicle. However, the person's head continues to move forwards and jerks the neck down, banging the chin onto the chest. The head then bounces back so that the face looks upwards. Even with time to tense the neck muscles, whiplash may not be prevented. An airbag in the vehicle, and a well-adjusted headrest on the seat, can hugely lessen its effects.

Despite warnings signs like this, many spinal injuries occur each year because people do not take enough care, and put their own bodies and health at risk.

Shallow water!

One cause of spinal cord injury, which can be prevented, is diving into water that is too shallow. The diver's head hits the bottom, or an obstruction, and is jerked up and back. This can smash the face and damage or even break the bones in the neck, and the spinal cord inside them. The result may be loss of feeling or movement below the neck.

FIRST AID FOR SPINE AND NERVE INJURIES

Suitable first aid for spinal or nerve injury can help to save lives and lessen long-term damage. However, unsuitable first aid can make the damage and disability worse, and can even be fatal.

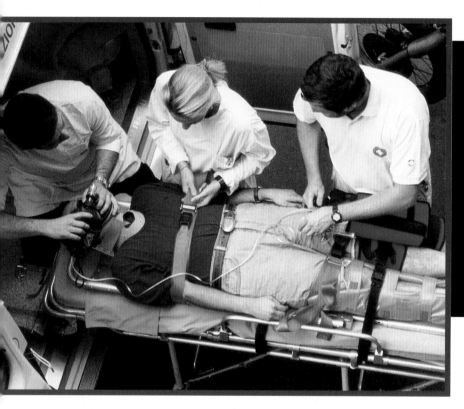

The spinal stretcher supports a casualty's head, neck and back, so that these do not move during the journey to hospital. However, putting the casualty into the stretcher is, in itself, a very skilled process to avoid nerve damage as the body parts are moved.

Saving the spinal cord

If the spinal cord is damaged, moving a casualty in the wrong way, or even at all, can increase the damage. As the casualty's neck or back is bent and twisted by movement, it can squash, press or cut the spinal cord. The same applies to other major nerves in the body and limbs.

The general advice in these situations is to leave the casualty in position, and avoid moving them. Usually, the casualty is moved only if her or his life is in danger, such as from fire, poisonous fumes, machines that are out of control or falling objects.

The key actions are:
- get expert help quickly – call a doctor, paramedic or ambulance
- make the casualty as warm and comfortable as possible
- support the casualty so that body parts cannot slip or move further
- stay calm and reassure the casualty.

Conscious and unconscious

When expert help arrives, a conscious casualty can be asked questions such as 'Can you feel your feet?' and 'Can you move your fingers?' The answers give clues to any nerve or spinal cord damage.

An expert will check an unconscious casualty's heartbeat, breathing and other signs. The expert may also check the casualty's **reflex** actions, and feel if various muscles are tensed or floppy. The results of these tests can suggest the site of any nerve or spinal cord injury.

Transport

If there is a risk of nerve or spinal cord damage, the casualty is transported with great care. Supports, such as splints, are used to prevent further damage. A neck or back injury is supported by a neck collar or back brace. The casualty may also be strapped into a spinal stretcher, which supports the whole body.

Later, in hospital, medical scans and **X-rays** are used to check for injury. Ordinary X-rays show mainly bones. Scans show nerves, **blood vessels** and other soft parts clearly.

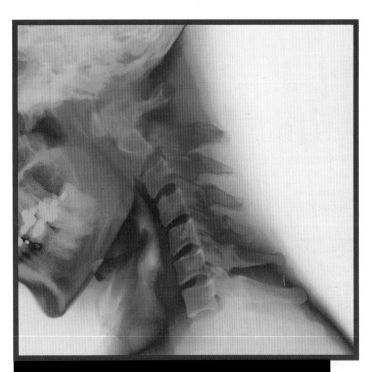

This X-ray image (colour-coded by computer) shows a broken neck. The two uppermost vertebrae or backbones, under the base of the skull behind the jaw, are moved out of position or dislocated, and the second one is fractured.

Referred pain

Sometimes, pain is felt in one part of the body when the actual damage is some distance away. This is called referred pain. For example, the heart may suffer a temporary lack of oxygen, if a person has angina. Yet the pain seems to come from the left shoulder or left arm.

It is thought that as nerve messages for pain arrive at the spinal cord, they get 'mixed up' with signals coming from elsewhere. The brain often thinks that the messages have come from the skin, since discomfort and pain usually happen here, rather than from parts deep inside the body.

The effect of a spinal cord injury depends largely on the level of the injury – whether high up in the neck, in the chest or lower in the back. Since the spinal cord carries **sensory** nerves going up to the brain and **motor** nerves coming back down, both feelings and movements can be affected.

Sensory nerve damage leads to numbness (lack of feeling), and perhaps aches, tingling or pain. Motor nerve damage causes muscle weakness or **paralysis** – the inability to move a body part. Either, or both, types of damage lead to loss of reflexes. The long-term outlook depends mainly on how much damage has been done.

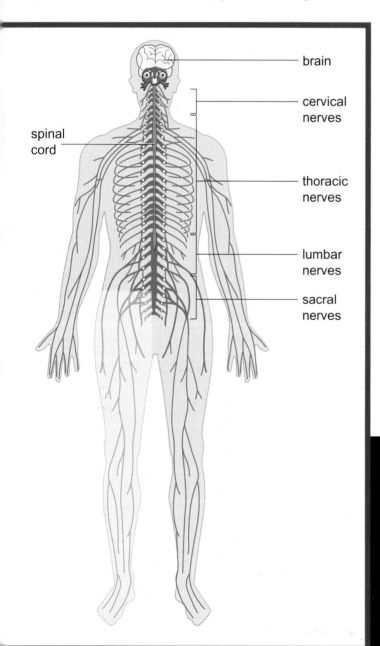

brain

cervical nerves

spinal cord

thoracic nerves

lumbar nerves

sacral nerves

Levels of injury

In general, a spinal cord injury affects the parts of the body below its level. So if damage occurs in the lower back, numbness and paralysis tend to affect the lower body and legs. This is known as paraplegia. It may include loss of control of the bladder and bowels, as well as no feeling in the skin, and the inability to walk.

If an injury occurs in the lower neck, the numbness and paralysis may affect all four limbs, which is known as quadriplegia or tetraplegia. It is sometimes also called 'paralysis from the neck down'.

In an accident, the spinal cord and nerves might be injured on the right side of the lowest or sacral region. This would affect the right hip, leg and foot, as shown. Damaged sensory nerves cause numbness, tingling or pain, while injured motor nerves prevent movement, which is known as paralysis.

An injury in the upper neck also affects the nerves that control breathing, which can be fatal. A patient injured here may recover, but might need assisted breathing with the help of a respirator. The real extent of a spinal injury may take days or weeks to become clear, because it is sometimes affected by spinal shock (see panel).

Long-term outlook

In some injuries, the spinal cord is swollen and bruised, but the nerve fibres are not broken. Usually, movements and feelings gradually return to the affected parts of the body. The injury recovers and the spinal cord heals, perhaps with the help of medication.

In other cases, surgery may be needed, to try to rejoin parts of the cord's nerve fibres. The aim is to get back some feeling and movement in the future. However, this type of surgery is extremely complex and delicate, and the patient usually takes a long time to recover. During rehabilitation, he or she may spend many difficult weeks re-learning actions that once seemed so simple, such as walking or holding a fork.

Spinal shock

In the hours and days after a spinal cord injury, spinal shock may develop. Bruising and swelling spread along the spinal cord, so that numbness, weakness or paralysis also spread – perhaps above the level of the injury, as well as below. In most cases, spinal shock gradually heals, but it can cause problems as doctors try to find out the real extent of the damage.

'Superman' actor Christopher Reeve has bravely battled severe spinal injury. He encourages other people with similar conditions to stay positive and keep progressing in recovery.

SPINAL CORD AND NERVE INFECTIONS

Germs (harmful **microbes**) can invade the spinal cord and nerves, either by infection of the area itself, or as part of infection elsewhere in the body. **Bacterial** germs can generally be attacked with **antibiotic** drugs to treat the infection. Antibiotics rarely affect viral germs, but they can be treated with a growing range of antiviral medications.

Spinal meningitis

In a healthy person, the cerebrospinal fluid around the brain and spinal cord is clear and watery. In some infections, it becomes milky or cloudy. This occurs especially in meningitis, which is the swelling of the **meninges** layers around the brain and cord. Spinal meningitis is usually due to an infection spreading from elsewhere. Rarer causes are a deep wound into the spinal cord, such as from a knife, bullet or severe accident.

If meningitis begins around the spinal cord, it may rapidly spread to the brain, as cerebral meningitis. Symptoms include a stiff neck and back, fever, nausea, vomiting, a severe headache and fear of, or pain from, bright lights. There may also be a reddish skin rash, which does not turn paler if the skin is pressed. Meningitis is a serious condition and needs urgent medical treatment.

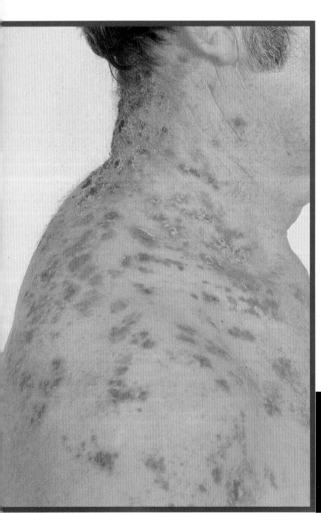

Shingles

Shingles usually follows chickenpox, when a type of herpes (*varicella*) virus causes very itchy blisters on the skin. Some viruses find their way to the nerve roots of the spinal cord and stay there, perhaps for years, causing no trouble. They may become active after another illness or perhaps emotional **stress**. This causes fever, intense, sharp pains along the nerve and an itchy red skin rash and blisters above the nerve. If shingles is discovered in time, it can be successfully treated with antiviral drugs.

Herpes viruses cause both the initial infection of chickenpox, with its itchy skin blisters, and then perhaps years later, shingles, which also has skin blisters and pain from the affected nerves.

Polio

Poliomyelitis has almost vanished from many parts of the world, due to vaccination (immunization) during childhood. However, outbreaks still occur. Polio viruses attack nerves in the lower brain and spinal cord, causing movement problems. There is also a sore throat, fever, bowel upsets and pains and weakness in the back, arms and legs. The affected muscles may go hard and tense, or become paralysed. With comfort and rest, most patients gradually recover from polio. In very rare cases, the paralysis remains.

Secondary effects

The spinal cord and **peripheral** nerves may be affected by germs that strike mainly at other body parts. These infections include rabies, syphilis, leprosy and diphtheria. HIV, the virus that causes AIDS, can also affect the spinal cord and nerves. It may cause a wide range of symptoms, including those described above.

In most regions of the world, the numbers of people with long-term disability after polio are reducing. This infection can cause life-long weakness or paralysis in a limb or body part; however, modern equipment can lessen the effects.

Tetanus

In tetanus, *Clostridium* bacteria multiply in various body parts, such as muscles. They make a poison, or **toxin**, that affects the spinal cord and nerves. The muscles controlled by these nerves, usually in the limbs and back, suffer cramps and **spasms** as they go hard and painful. This may happen in the face and jaw muscles, leading to a common name for tetanus, 'lockjaw'. If the chest and breathing muscles are involved, the infection may be fatal.

Tetanus is very rare in many regions due to immunization. Treatment includes powerful drugs, such as antitoxins, which make the toxins less harmful.

Various medical conditions can affect the spinal cord and nerves. They range from spina bifida, which occurs during a baby's development in the womb, to the effects of ageing on nerves, which make skin feelings less clear and muscle control less precise.

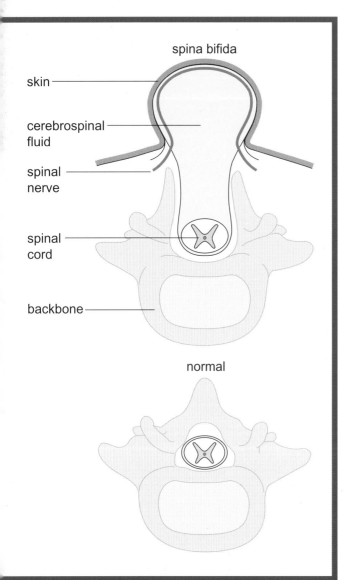

spina bifida

skin

cerebrospinal fluid

spinal nerve

spinal cord

backbone

normal

In spina bifida (top diagram) the vertebrae, or backbones, do not enclose the spinal cord fully, as they develop, in the womb. The spinal cord and meninges are not protected, as they are normally (bottom diagram). The meninges and cerebrospinal fluid may protrude through the gap of missing bone and form a bulge under the skin.

Spina bifida

In this **congenital** condition (present at birth), the backbone does not form properly during early development in the womb. The vertebral bones do not enclose the spinal cord. There is a gap along the rear of the backbone, which exposes the spinal cord. The cord itself may also be affected.

Spina bifida tends to run in families, due to a **genetic**, or inherited, problem. It is varied in its effects. In some cases, the affected part of the backbone is small. In others, it is more severe, and there is lack of feeling or control in the lower body, legs, bladder and bowel. The main treatment is an operation.

Peripheral nerve damage

Nerves can be damaged in many ways besides physical injury. These problems are known by various names, such as **peripheral** neuritis and peripheral neuropathy.

One type of damage is from harmful chemicals, called **toxins**, which somehow get into the body. They include certain pesticides, weedkillers, industrial chemicals such as lead, mercury, arsenic and cadmium, and also various non-medical drugs. Other cases of nerve damage are due to another condition, such as an infection, **tumour** (growth), long-term diabetes or an **autoimmune** disorder (see page 38).

Spinal or nerve problems are no bar to staying active and taking part in exercise and sports, including international and Olympic level.

Symptoms and treatment

In most cases, peripheral nerve damage is felt as a tingling sensation that gradually spreads, for example, from the fingers up the arm. This may be followed by numbness, muscle weakness and **paralysis**. In some cases, sharp pains shoot along the affected nerve, which is known as neuralgia.

The sooner any nerve damage is detected, the sooner treatment can begin. However it may not be possible to heal nerve damage that has already occurred.

Spinal tumours

Like any part of the body, **tumours** (growths) may occur in the spinal cord or nerves. Depending on the tumour's site and size, it can cause back pain, muscle weakness, loss of feeling, strange hot-and-cold sensations and loss of control of the bladder and bowels. The main treatment is surgery.

Self-inflicted nerve damage

Some cases of nerve damage are due to a person's behaviour or lifestyle. Alcohol or drug abuse, or an unhealthy diet with lack of vitamins and **minerals**, can affect the spinal cord and peripheral nerves. (Of course, it can have much more serious effects on the brain.) The resulting damage may cause weakness and paralysis, so the person cannot move around, and numbness, which brings the risk of further injury.

Guillain-Barre syndrome

Guillain-Barre syndrome is a sudden, severe attack of nerve damage. It may be brought on by a viral illness or, in very rare cases, by an immunization. The person may need intensive hospital treatment, especially if breathing is affected. In most instances, the person gradually recovers.

Multiple sclerosis (MS) is usually a long-term condition that affects nerve **cells**. In particular, it affects the outer coverings, or **myelin** sheaths, of their fibres. It is usually due to an **autoimmune** problem. This means that the body's **immune system**, which normally fights against germs and other invaders to protect against disease, goes wrong. It turns against its own cells and parts and attacks them.

The immune system

In multiple sclerosis, white blood cells, known as T-cells (which are part of the immune system), act in a faulty way. They attack a substance, called myelin (basic protein), which is found in the myelin sheath around each nerve fibre. This damages the myelin and the cells that make it. Nerve messages cannot pass normally along the fibre.

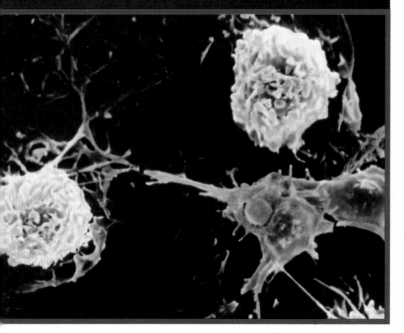

In multiple sclerosis, the myelin sheaths around nerve fibres are damaged. This may occur because cells called oligodendrocytes (shown here in purple), which help to form and nourish the myelin, are attacked by the body's own defence system (yellow cells).

After several attacks, the myelin and fibres are stiffened, or 'sclerosed', by hard, scar-like material. The nerve cell may not be able to send any nerve messages.

Effects of multiple sclerosis

Multiple sclerosis can affect a few or many body parts. In **sensory** nerves, it causes strange sensations, such as tingling and numbness. In **motor** nerves, it leads to loss of muscle power and coordination, and perhaps loss of bladder and bowel control. Multiple sclerosis may disappear after one attack, or come back more severely each time.

Multiple sclerosis affects about one person in 700–1000. However, this varies greatly among different ethnic groups, and it also depends partly on where a person lives – and where he or she grew up. The condition tends to begin at the age of about 20 to 30 years, and it tends to run in some families. It may be set off, or triggered, by a viral infection, possibly such as measles or herpes. There are many forms of treatment, depending on how the individual person is affected.

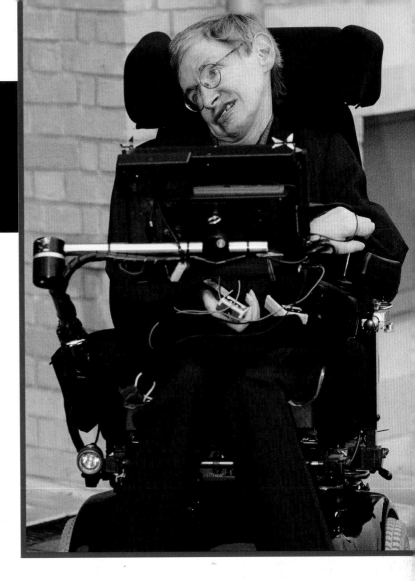

Stephen Hawking is one of the world's most famous and respected scientists, despite a nerve disorder that restricts his speech and other movements.

Motor neuron disease

Motor neuron disease (MND) causes damage to motor nerve cells that carry messages from the brain out to muscles. There are various forms of the disease. In amyotrophic lateral sclerosis (ALS), motor nerve cells in the brain and spinal cord are affected. The muscles they control, especially in the hands, and those used for breathing, speaking, chewing and swallowing, become weak and waste away.

All types of motor neuron disease are rare, and a few run in families. However, the causes are not clear. Most cases begin after the age of 50 years, and take several years to progress. There is no standard, effective treatment.

Myasthenia gravis

Myasthenia gravis (MG) affects the workings of the **neurotransmitter** acetylcholine, as mentioned on page 13. This chemical passes messages between nerve cells, especially in the **peripheral** nervous system. Myasthenia gravis is an autoimmune disorder that attacks the places where acetylcholine has its effect, on the cell **membranes** of nerve cells and muscle cells. As a result, the affected muscles become weak and poorly controlled – from a drooping eyelid to difficulty in breathing. There are various treatments, including drugs and surgery.

DRUGS AND THE NERVOUS SYSTEM

The nervous system is based on body chemicals. Even its tiny electrical pulses, which represent nerve messages, are made by moving chemicals. This is why more chemicals, in the form of medical drugs, can be useful to treat disorders of the nervous system. Many of these drugs affect the central nervous system – the brain and spinal cord. Fewer have their main actions on **peripheral** nerves.

Stimulants

A **stimulant** increases activity of the nervous system, making the body more tense and ready for action. The person has greater awareness, and perhaps temporary feelings of alertness and well-being. Much of this stimulant effect is due to extra activity in the sympathetic part of the **autonomic** nervous system, as described on page 27.

Mild stimulants include caffeine in tea, coffee and cola drinks, and nicotine in tobacco. More powerful stimulants are amphetamines ('uppers'), benzedrine and methedrine ('speed').

Depressants

A depressant drug does not necessarily cause feelings of depression, sadness and hopelessness. It depresses, or slows down, nervous system activity. Its effects are generally opposite to those of a stimulant. They include relief of tension, anxiety and worry (which may bring on temporary feelings of well-being), as well as drowsiness and, perhaps, confusion.

Tooth care might be more uncomfortable, if we did not have anaesthetic drugs that dull nerve sensations so that we feel no pain.

Most depressants act on the brain. Alcohol (ethyl alcohol) affects the action of acetylcholine and other **neurotransmitters**. Some **tranquillizer** drugs also do this.

Some depressants are addictive, so a person needs to keep taking them. In larger doses, many depressants cause harmful reactions and nervous system damage.

Painkillers

Painkillers (**analgesics**) relieve, or 'kill', pain sensations, and work mainly within the central nervous system, including the spinal cord. There are two main groups: non-opiates (non-opioid), and opiates (opioids). Many opiates/opioids are derived from natural sources, such as plants. They include codeine, methadone and morphine. These help to reduce the numbers of nerve messages about pain being sent up the spinal cord to the brain.

The body produces its own opiate-like painkillers, known as endorphins. These can have the same effect on the spinal cord and brain as opiates. If the body is under great **stress** or danger, yet also in pain, its endorphins can help to damp down the pain, while the stress and danger are dealt with.

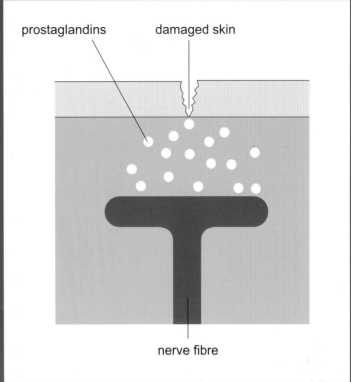

When part of the body is injured, such as a cut in the skin, the damaged cells release natural chemicals called prostaglandins. These affect nerve endings and cause signals that are sent to the brain, where they are experienced as pain. Some painkilling medications work by preventing prostaglandins from having this effect.

Prostaglandins

Prostaglandins are natural body substances that are similar to **hormones**. Some affect the ways that nerve processes work. There are dozens of kinds of prostaglandins, made in many parts of the body, and with many different effects. Some are made when a body part is damaged. They help to send pain signals along peripheral nerves, so that the brain is warned of the harm. The familiar painkilling drug aspirin works partly by stopping these prostaglandins.

HELPING THE NERVOUS SYSTEM TO HEALTH

The nervous system is very delicate and specialized. In some cases, injury cannot be repaired, nor disease healed. However, recent progress in medical drugs and surgery is leading to better treatments and outlook for millions of people.

Neurosurgery

A single nerve **cell** with its **fibre** is too small to see with the unaided eye. An operating magnifier or microscope allows a surgeon to see tiny bundles of nerves. Using especially small instruments, such as scalpels (sharp blades) and forceps (tweezers), the surgeon can operate on nerves with amazing skill. Laser scalpels are often used, since the laser beam can be aimed very precisely to cut and heat-seal tiny areas.

These methods are used to join back, or reattach, body parts that have been cut off during an accident. Such operations are long and complex. Different medical teams rejoin nerves as well as **blood vessels**, muscles, tendons and other parts. If the nerves are rejoined successfully, the part may be able to recover some feeling and movement. However, as the nerve **fibres** connect, they may not make the same links as before. This alters the nerve pathways that were familiar to the brain. The person may have to 're-train' both the brain and nerves, and gradually 're-learn' movement skills.

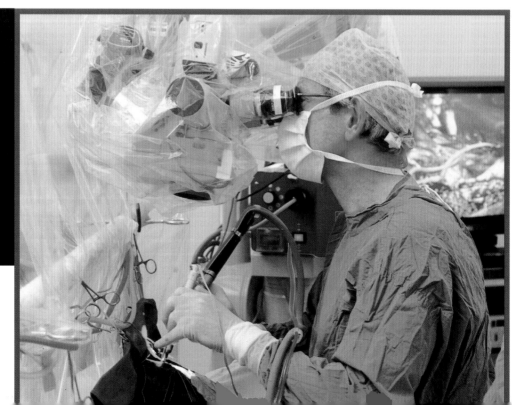

Nerve surgery is greatly helped by operating microscopes, so the surgeon can see and work on individual nerve fibres.

Nerve-growing chemicals

If a **peripheral** nerve is cut or damaged, the individual nerve cells may regrow parts of themselves. This natural repair can take weeks or months, if it happens at all. It is even slower, and often less successful, in the spinal cord.

However, this nerve repair can be made faster and more successful by substances called nerve-growth (neurotrophic) factors. Some of these have been discovered by studies on the nervous system when it is rapidly developing, early in life. Others have been found by tests on nerve cells that have been grown outside of the body, in the laboratory. The nerve-growth chemicals encourage nerve cells to send out new **dendrites** and fibres, and to make new connections.

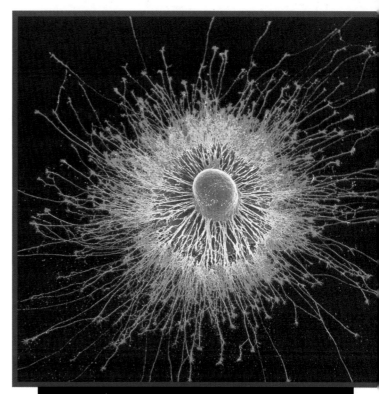

This coloured electron micrograph scan shows a piece of spinal cord with the axons (nerve fibres) around it.

New nerve cells for old

A recent area of research for problems of the nervous system (and other body systems) is the use of stem cells. These are cells that have not yet become specialized to do a certain job. One day, some stem cells, perhaps from the umbilical cords of new babies, may be able to be grown to specialize into nerve cells. They could replace nerve cells lost by injury or disease.

The most vital system

All parts and systems of the body are important, but the spinal cord and nerves are especially so. They carry information throughout the body, and to and from the brain. Nerves control and coordinate many processes and parts inside the body, which keep us alive and healthy. They also bring information from the senses to the brain, so that we can see, hear and feel our surroundings, and smell and taste our food. Nerves also carry information away from the brain to the muscles, so that we can carry out a vast array of actions and movements, from breathing, eating and writing, to running, jumping and playing sports.

WHAT CAN GO WRONG WITH MY SPINAL CORD AND NERVOUS SYSTEM?

This book explains the different parts of the nervous system (apart from the brain), how they work, and how they may be damaged by injury and illness. This page summarizes some of the problems that can affect the nerves and spinal cord, especially in young people. It also gives you information about how each problem is treated.

Many problems can be avoided by simple, practical health measures such as taking regular exercise, getting plenty of rest, eating a balanced diet and taking care with high-risk activities. This page shows some of the ways you can prevent injury and illness.

Remember, if you think something is wrong with your body, you should always talk to a trained medical professional, like a doctor or a school nurse. Regular medical check-ups are another important part of staying healthy in body and mind.

Condition	Cause	Symptoms	Prevention	Treatment
prolapsed or 'slipped' disc	the cartilage disc between two vertebral bones may be weak or injured, and a bulge or prolapse presses on a spinal nerve or on the cord itself	pain, at the site of the bulge in the neck or back, and perhaps in the parts connected by that nerve, along with numbness and weakness in those parts	measures to prevent injury to the neck or back, including protective equipment in risky sports or hazardous pursuits, always wearing a seat belt in vehicles, also lifting and carrying heavy loads correctly or asking for help	rest, pain-reliever medication, physical therapies including physiotherapy, chiropractic and specific exercises; in some cases, an operation
spinal meningitis	infection by germs such as bacteria or viruses spreading from elsewhere, or entering through a deep wound into the cord	stiff neck and back, fever, nausea, vomiting, severe headache, extreme sensitivity or pain from bright light, reddish skin rash	general precautions to prevent neck and back injury, especially a penetrating wound from sharp objects. Wear protective and safety equipment.	be seen by a doctor urgently for antibiotic or similar drugs, nursing care and support

Condition	Cause	Symptoms	Prevention	Treatment
carpal tunnel syndrome	pressure on the median nerve in the wrist due to injury, a disorder that affects the joints such as arthritis, repeated wrist/finger movements such as certain computer operations, or hormonal changes in the female body, especially in middle age	tingling and numbness in parts of the hand, pain that is worse at night because the body is inactive and the pressure on the nerve is not relieved or shifted by movement	protect the wrist from injury with suitable clothing or guards, also avoid repetitive wrist and hand movements, resting and stretching the hand and fingers regularly	rest, anti-inflammatory drugs as tablets or by injection, or loosening the carpal ligament by an operation; of the alternative therapies, acupuncture is found to be effective
spinal cord injury	neck or back damage due to traffic accident, fall, high-speed collision, diving into too-shallow water or similar physical injury	vary greatly depending on site and severity of damage, from pain and numbness in an arm or leg, to numbness and paralysis of whole body below neck	protect neck and back at all times, including wearing seat belts in vehicles, taking care on ladders or where falls are a risk, using protective equipment in hazardous sports or pursuits	depends on severity – emergency expert care for first aid and transport, rest and pain-reliever medication, possibly surgery, physiotherapy and specific exercises, perhaps long-term mobility aids
shingles	infection by a type of herpes (*varicella*) virus, usually following chickenpox	fever, intense sharp pains along a nerve, itchy red skin rash and blisters above the nerve	general measures for good health, coping well with severe stress and emotional upset	antiviral drugs, rest, pain-relievers, lotion or cream to reduce blistering and inflammation

 MORE BOOKS TO READ

The Human Machine: The Controls, Sarah Angliss (Belitha Press, 2002)

Look at Your Body: Brain and Nerves, Steve Parker (Franklin Watts, 2002)

GLOSSARY

analgesic pain-reducing, pain-relieving painkiller

anti-inflammatory reducing inflammation (swelling, redness, soreness and, perhaps, pain)

antibiotic type of medical drug that kills bacteria

autoimmune when the body's immune system goes wrong, and harms its own cells and parts

autonomic able to work on its own or carry out actions by itself

axon long, thin part or fibre that carries nerve signals away from a nerve cell body

bacteria group of micro-organisms that can cause infections

blood vessels network of tubes that carry blood around the body

cartilage tough, strong, slightly bendy body substance, sometimes called 'gristle'

cell microscopic unit, or 'building block', of a living thing – the body is made of billions of cells

cell body main part of a cell

congenital present at birth

dendrites thin, branching parts that carry nerve signals towards a nerve cell

fibrous made of stringy or thread-like parts (fibres)

gamma globulin substances in the blood, some made ↴ fight invading germs

ganglia lump-like bulges, especially along nerves

genetic to do with genes, which are the instructions for life and exist as the genetic material, DNA

gland body part that makes and releases a product (usually a liquid), such as a hormone

haemorrhage leak of blood, bleeding

homeostasis keeping conditions inside the body constant and stable

hormone natural chemical substance, which affects the workings of specific body parts

hypothalamus small part of the brain concerned with vital life functions, with close links to the hormone system

immune system body's defence mechanisms against infection and disease

inherited passed from parents to offspring

involuntary happening without the need for us think or decide about it, and that we cannot control 'at will'

ion tiny particle of a substance, such as a mineral, which is positive or negative

membrane sheet- or skin-like covering or lining layer

meninges three layers of membranes wrapped around the spinal cord and brain

microbe very small living thing, only visible under a microscope

mineral one of a number of chemicals needed by the body in very small amounts, for example, calcium and iron

motor to do with muscles and the movements they make

myelin fatty substance wrapped around certain nerve fibres

neurotransmitter chemical substance that passes a nerve message from one nerve cell to the next, across the junction (synapse)

nucleus central part of a cell, containing the genetic material, DNA

paralysis inability to move

peripheral around the edge, away from the middle or centre

receptor place or site which receives or accepts a specific substance, like a lock which receives a key

reflex body reaction that occurs quickly and automatically, in response to a certain action

sensory to do with detecting or sensing conditions, substances or energy, such as the eyes, which sense light rays

spasm when muscles pull or contract without warning, not in a controlled way

stimulant substance that stimulates or speeds up, increasing activity

stress adverse, difficult or challenging conditions, from physical fatigue or lack of food to emotional worry

synapse junction or join between two nerve cells, where they are separated by a tiny gap

toxin harmful or poisonous substance

tranquillizer substance that slows down the body's activity

tumour lump-like abnormal growth or swelling, which may or may not be malignant (cancerous)

virus very small micro-organism that can cause infection

voluntary happening only after we think or decide to do it, and which we can control 'at will'

X-rays form of energy, as rays or radiation, which pass through soft body parts such as flesh, but that are stopped by hard parts like bones

INDEX